THE NUTCRACKERS
AND THE SUGAR-TONGS

THE NUTCRACKERS

AND THE SUGAR-TONGS

by Edward Lear

Illustrated by
Marcia Sewall

An Atlantic Monthly Press Book
BOSTON Little, Brown and Company TORONTO

Illustrated by Marcia Sewall

MASTER OF ALL MASTERS
THE SQUIRE'S BRIDE
THE PARROT AND THE THIEF
THE PORCELAIN MAN
COME AGAIN IN THE SPRING
COO-MY-DOVE, MY DEAR
THE WEE, WEE MANNIE AND THE BIG, BIG COO
THE NUTCRACKERS AND THE SUGAR-TONGS

ILLUSTRATIONS COPYRIGHT © 1978 BY MARCIA SEWALL

FIRST EDITION

T 03/78

Library of Congress Cataloging in Publication Data

Lear, Edward, 1812–1888.
   The nutcrackers and the sugar-tongs.

   "An Atlantic Monthly Press book."
   SUMMARY: The nutcrackers and sugar-tongs suddenly
decide to leave their place at the table and go off on
horses, leaving the household behind in chaos and confusion.
   [1. Nonsense verses]   I. Sewall, Marcia.   II. Title.
PZ8. 3.L477Nu 1978   821'.8   77-12696
ISBN 0-316-78181-9

ATLANTIC–LITTLE, BROWN BOOKS
ARE PUBLISHED BY
LITTLE, BROWN AND COMPANY
IN ASSOCIATION WITH
THE ATLANTIC MONTHLY PRESS

*Published simultaneously in Canada
by Little, Brown & Company (Canada) Limited*

PRINTED IN THE UNITED STATES OF AMERICA

For Edgar and Alice

The Nutcrackers sat by a plate on the table,

The Sugar-tongs sat by a plate at his side;

And the Nutcrackers said, "Don't you wish we were able
    Along the blue hills and the green meadows to ride?
Must we drag on this stupid existence forever,
    So idle and weary, so full of remorse,
While everyone else takes his pleasure, and never
    Seems happy unless he is riding a horse?

Don't you think we could ride without being instructed?

　Without any saddle, or bridle, or spur?

Our legs are so long, and so aptly constructed,

　I'm sure that an accident could not occur.

Let us all of a sudden hop down from the table,

　And hustle downstairs, and each jump on a horse!

Shall we try? Shall we go? Do you think we are able?"

　The Sugar-tongs answered distinctly, "Of course!"

So down the long staircase they hopped in a minute,
  The Sugar-tongs snapped, and the Crackers said, "Crack!"

The stable was open, the horses were in it;

Each took out a pony, and jumped on his back.

The Cat in a fright scrambled out of the doorway,
The Mice tumbled out of a bundle of hay,

The brown and white Rats, and the black ones from Norway

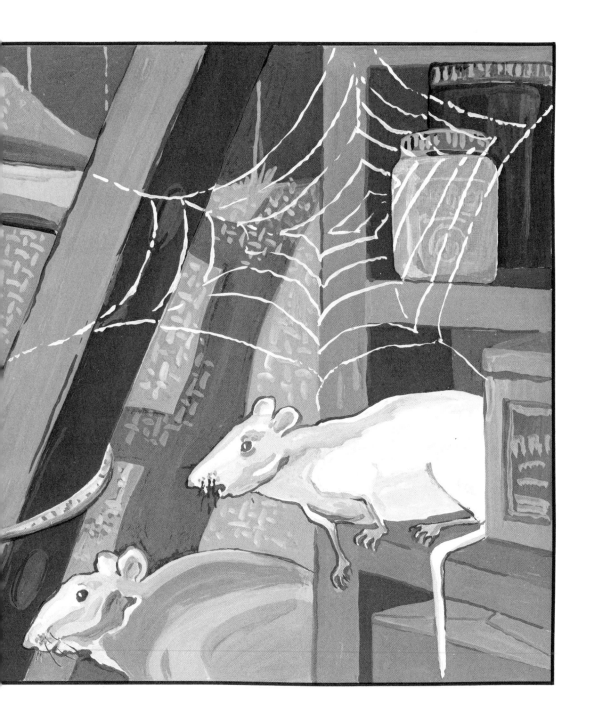

Screamed out, "They are taking the horses away!"

The whole of the household was filled with amazement,
The Cups and the Saucers danced madly about,
The Plates and the Dishes looked out of the casement,
The Saltcellar stood on his head with a shout,

The Spoons with a clatter looked out of the lattice,
The Mustard-pot climbed up the Gooseberry Pies,

The Soup-ladle peeped through a heap of Veal Patties,
And squeaked with a ladle-like scream of surprise.

The Frying-pan said, "It's an awful delusion!"
The Tea-kettle hissed and grew black in the face;

And they all rushed downstairs in the wildest confusion,

To see the great Nutcracker–Sugar-tong race.

And out of the stable, with screamings and laughter
   (Their ponies were cream-colored, speckled with brown),
The Nutcrackers first, and the Sugar-tongs after,
   Rode all round the yard, and then all round the town.

They rode through the street, and they rode by the station,
They galloped away to the beautiful shore;
In silence they rode, and "made no observation,"
Save this: "We will never go back anymore!"

And still you might hear, till they rode out of hearing,
  The Sugar-tongs snap, and the Crackers say, "Crack!"

Till far in the distance, their forms disappearing,
They faded away. — And they never came back!